Computers

CHRISTINE TAYLOR-BUTLER

Children's Press®
An Imprint of Scholastic Inc.

Content Consultant
Dale F. Reed, PhD
Department of Computer Science
University of Illinois at Chicago, Chicago, Illinois

Library of Congress Cataloging-in-Publication Data
Names: Taylor-Butler, Christine, author.
Title: Computers / Christine Taylor-Butler.
Other titles: True book.
Description: New York : Children's Press, an imprint of Scholastic Inc., [2017] | Series: A true book
  | Includes bibliographical references and index.
Identifiers: LCCN 2016000348| ISBN 9780531218624 (library binding) | ISBN 9780531227800 (pbk.)
Subjects: LCSH: Computers—Juvenile literature. | Computers—History—Juvenile literature.
Classification: LCC QA76.23 .T39 2017 | DDC 004—dc23
LC record available at http://lccn.loc.gov/2016000348

Front cover: An illustration of
a robot reading a book

Back cover: A young girl assembling
an electronic circuit

Find the Truth!

Everything you are about to read is true *except* for one of the sentences on this page.

Which one is **TRUE**?

T or F Microsoft invented the first personal computers.

T or F Early computers once filled an entire room.

Find the answers in this book.

3

Contents

THE **BIG** TRUTH!

Computer Graphics Through the Years

Virtual reality

The Micro Mote
computer

Tablet computer

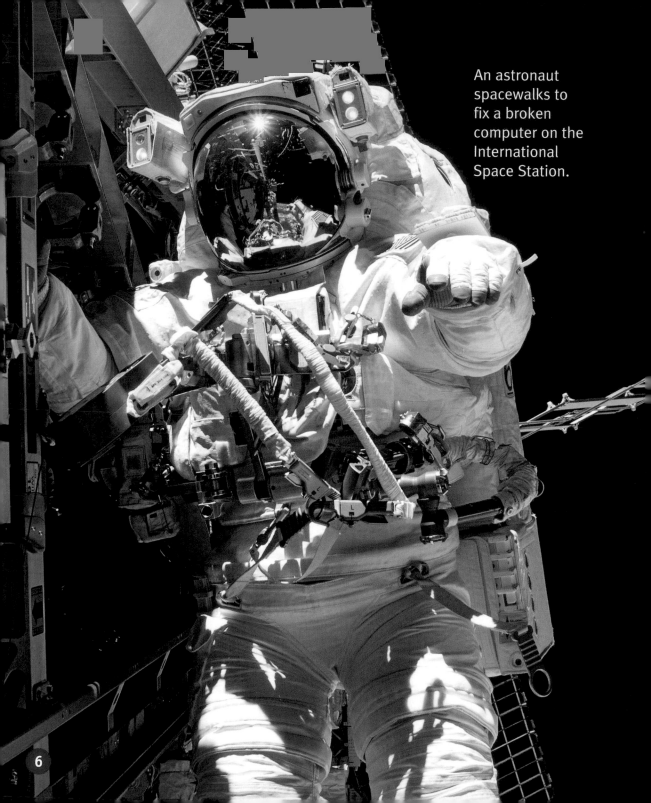

An astronaut
spacewalks to
fix a broken
computer on the
International
Space Station.

The First Steps

How many times have you used a computer today? Maybe you watched a video or looked up information for a school project. These powerful devices are everywhere. Computers make many complex tasks easier. They might be used for something as simple as typing and storing a document. But they can also be used for something as complicated as sending a spacecraft, such as the Mars Rover, to Mars.

The Mars Rover transmits data from 140 million miles (225 million km) away.

Mechanical Math Machines

Before we had computers, people built mechanical devices to help solve math problems. These devices worked without electricity. One of the earliest known math machines was created thousands of years ago. Called an abacus, it used rows of beads to perform math computations. Another device, the slide rule, was developed in the 1600s. It could multiply and divide and even solve **trigonometry** problems.

NASA scientists used slide rules when designing the space program.

As knowledge of the world grew, the problems scientists wanted to solve became more complex. Something faster and more sophisticated was needed. In 1822, Charles Babbage set out to design a

Charles Babbage's designs helped lead to the creation of the earliest modern computers.

"Difference" machine that could calculate and print math tables. Punch cards would be used to **input** data into the machine. The machine would be 7 feet (2.1 meters) tall and weigh 5 tons. It required wheels, gears, and cranks to work.

Babbage's machines were finally built after his death.

The British government became interested in funding Babbage's machine. However, the complicated design required 25,000 hand-built parts. While craftsmen created tools necessary to build them, Babbage designed an even larger "Analytical" machine. He was able to build only a small demonstration model. By then the government had lost interest.

Turing's Triumph

During World War II, the British government was working to decode secret messages sent by the German military. The government recruited math expert Alan Turing to help. The German messages were created on a typewriter-like device called the Enigma machine, which

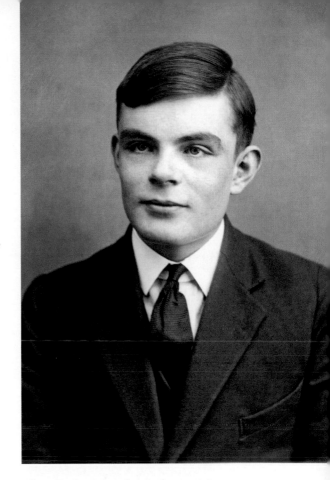

Alan Turing worked alongside a team of fellow code breakers during World War II.

scrambled the letters. The British military worked around the clock to crack the Enigma's code, but the code changed every day at midnight.

A working replica of Turing's machine can be found in Bletchley Park Museum in England.

In 1939, Turing perfected a computer that could break codes faster than a human could. The machine, called a bombe, was 7 feet (2 m) wide and more than 6 feet (1.8 m) tall. It was partially mechanical and partially electronic. Its 108 color-coded **rotors** were attached to a motor. More than 200 bombes were built to help figure out Germany's plans during the war.

Colossus

By 1944, Great Britain had developed the first programmable computer. Invented by engineer Tommy Flowers, the Colossus was even larger than Turing's bombe. It was powered by 1,500 electronic vacuum tubes. A second version had 2,400 tubes. The tubes "read" information from a paper tape using light. This information was then stored inside the machine. The computer was programmed using plugs, wires, and switches.

The Colossus was kept secret until the 1970s.

13

ENIAC was used to calculate the speed and path of missiles and bombs.

ENIAC cost $500,000 to build.

The Enormous ENIAC

The U.S. Army created its own secret computer in 1946. The Electronic Numerical Integrator And Computer (ENIAC) required 18,000 vacuum tubes, 6,000 cables, and thousands of other parts. It weighed 30 tons. Calculations that took 12 hours for a human to complete could be done in 30 seconds using ENIAC.

Paving the Way

The word *computer* once referred to the people who programmed computing machines. Women who held math degrees programmed many of the early machines, including ENIAC. They learned how to program the top secret machines without manuals or teachers. Without these women, World War II might have had a different outcome.

Scientists John Bardeen (standing left), Walter Brattain (standing right), and William Shockley (seated) helped make computers smaller with their discoveries.

The Blueprints for Modern Computers

Early computers were hard to maintain and not practical for most businesses. Their bulky vacuum tubes controlled the flow of electricity. That made them useful as switches. But vacuum tubes are a lot like old-fashioned lightbulbs. They eventually fail after a great deal of use. On average, one of ENIAC's tubes failed every other day. Computers needed to become smaller and more practical.

Vacuum tubes used light to create binary code for programming. 0 = off and 1 = on.

It's Electric

In 1947, scientists at Bell Laboratories created a new type of **semiconductor** material called a transistor. Transistors act as switches that can stop and start an electrical signal. They can also control how much current flows through them. Engineers soon began to use transistors, instead of bulky vacuum tubes, to build computers.

The first semiconductor was created by Michael Faraday in 1833.

Bardeen, Brattain, and Shockley received the 1956 Nobel Prize in Physics for their invention of the transistor.

Punch cards were used as early as 1725 to control machines that wove fabric.

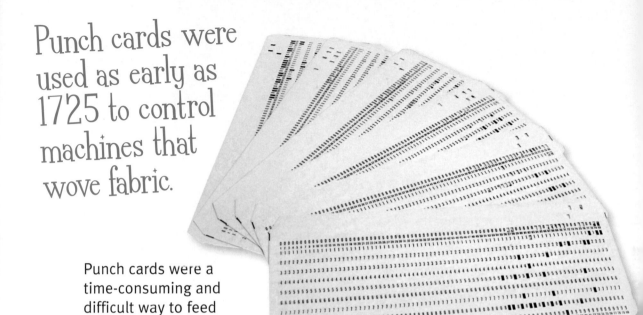

Punch cards were a time-consuming and difficult way to feed data into computers.

Dealing With Data

Engineers also looked for new ways to store information and give instructions to computers. Many early computers used punch cards. These cards were inserted into a computer. The computer then read the patterns of holes on the cards. Beginning in the 1950s, the use of magnetic tapes in computers made it easier to input and store data.

The BASIC programming language made it much easier to create instructions for computers.

Speaking a Different Language

The methods for programming early computers were often very complicated and hard to use. In 1964, John Kemeny and Thomas Kurtz invented a **programming language** called BASIC. It was much easier to use than previous computer languages. Businesses and consumers alike used it to create useful programs for their computers.

Smaller and Smaller

The last roadblock to making smaller computers was the size of **integrated circuits**, known as chips. Newer computers needed a separate chip for every function. In 1971, engineer Ted Hoff created the first microprocessor chip. The chip was less than an inch long (2.5 centimeters) but could run programs, store information, and process data all at the same time.

Microprocessor chips are made of silicon.

Early PCs were much larger and less powerful than the ones we use today.

COMPUTER BASIC
 7167 BYTES FREE
DISK READY.

CHAPTER 3

Getting Personal

As computers became smaller and more powerful, more people began using them. By the 1960s, companies such as International Business Machines (IBM) found success selling powerful computer systems to businesses. These computers were still used mainly by experts for work purposes. However, the personal computer (PC) was about to change everything.

IBM's first portable computer weighed 55 pounds (25 kilograms) and cost $9,000.

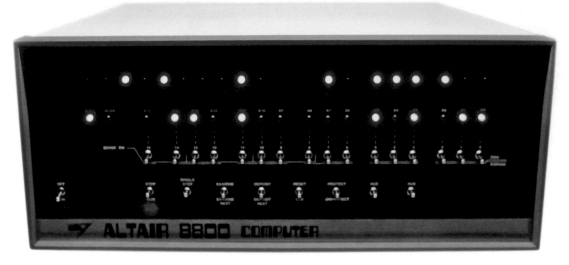

The Altair computer was introduced in 1975.

A Growing Interest

During the 1960s and 1970s, many talented engineers began working with computers as a hobby. Some built computers of their own design. Others built machines from kits. One popular kit computer was the Altair. These computers lacked monitors, keyboards, or other modern attachments. Instead, they had a panel of blinking lights and switches that were used to input programs.

The Two Steves

In the mid-1970s, two California computer hobbyists, Steve Jobs and Steve Wozniak, formed a company called Apple. Their Apple II computer, released in 1977, came with a built-in monitor and keyboard. It also offered color graphics and a variety of useful programs. These features made it one of the first computers to catch on with users who were not computer experts.

The region of California where many high-tech computer companies are found is nicknamed Silicon Valley.

Steve Wozniak (left) and Steve Jobs (right) pose with one of their early creations.

The Making of Microsoft

Paul Allen and Bill Gates were hired to modify BASIC for use with the Altair. Soon after, they formed Microsoft. Their corporation modified the widely used DOS **software** to work with IBM computers. MS-DOS made it easier for consumers to use PC computers. The Windows **operating system** was introduced two years later. By the 1980s, Microsoft software was used worldwide.

Microsoft's Paul Allen (left) and Bill Gates (right) helped make PCs popular with their powerful, yet easy-to-use, software.

Seymour Cray shows off one of his supercomputer designs in 1982.

The Biggest and Best

Even as PCs became more popular, businesses and militaries still had a need for massive **supercomputers**. Supercomputer pioneer Seymour Cray introduced the Cray-1 in 1976. The Cray-1 cost $8.8 million to build and performed 160 million calculations per second. How does that compare to today's supercomputers? Modern Cray machines are around 145,000 times faster than the original Cray-1!

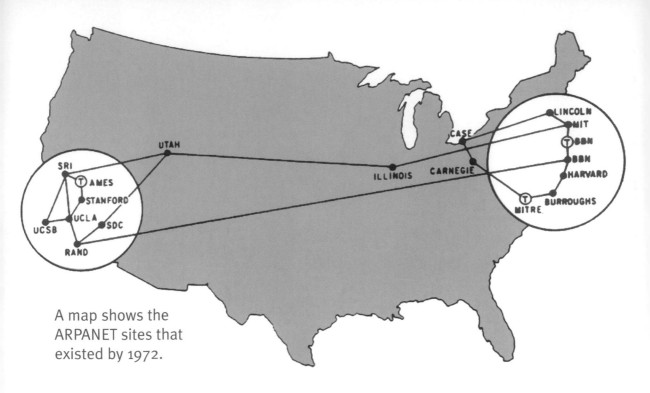

A map shows the ARPANET sites that existed by 1972.

From the ARPANET to the Internet

Today, it is hard to imagine using computers without the Internet. The Internet began with the creation of the Advanced Research Projects Agency **Network** (ARPANET) in 1969. At first, this network connected computers at four universities in the United States. Over time, it grew to include more and more computers. Users could send e-mails to each other and share computer files.

ARPANET was first used by scientists and government organizations. Internet protocol (IP) addresses were used to route information. As personal computers became popular during the 1980s, many companies began offering online services to everyday people. By the late 1990s, internet service providers (ISPs) were connecting tens of millions of people to the global network. Hypertext Transfer Protocol (HTTP) routes the data to the target computer.

Today, the Internet is an important part of everyday life for millions of people.

Computer Graphics

Early computers could show little more than plain green or white text on a black screen. But computer graphics have come a long way since then.

Before computers were able to display photos and other graphics, some clever users arranged letters, numbers, and punctuation marks to create pictures like the one shown here.

The Apple II, released in 1977, was one of the first widely available computers to display color graphics. Around the same time, some of the first home video game systems with color graphics were also released! At first, computers could only show a few colors at a time. Images were blocky. Over time, they were able to show more colors. Digital images became more detailed.

Through the Years

Today's devices can display realistic 3-D graphics. Powerful graphics cards are able to create entire worlds filled with expressive characters. This technology is used to create everything from video games to animated movies.

Virtual reality devices are also growing in popularity. Users wear a set of goggles that plug into a computer. They then see a 3-D world. To look around, all the user has to do is move his or her head.

You probably use computers every day, whether it is to do your homework or watch videos online.

Computers Everywhere

By the 2000s, PCs had become a part of everyday life for many people. People used them in business, education, entertainment, and everything in between. As a result, a new generation of engineers and programmers worked to continue improving the devices. Computers became even smaller, faster, and easier to use.

Cellphones are more powerful than computers used for NASA's Apollo moon missions.

Many young people use their smartphones more for texting than for phone calls.

On the Go

Today's computers are extremely small and portable. Most users no longer need big machines that cover an entire desk. Instead, many people carry computers everywhere they go. Laptops, smartphones, and tablets are all types of computers.

The Tiniest Computer Yet

The smallest computer yet is more than just portable. The Micro Mote computer, designed at the University of Michigan, is about the size of a single grain of rice. It is powered using sunlight. The Micro Mote's inventors hope that the tiny device could one day be used for everything from medical procedures to measuring air and water pollution. These abilities can make computers an important part of protecting our health, environment, and other aspects of our lives.

Up in the Cloud

Cloud computing makes it easier than ever before to use a computer anywhere you go. Files are stored not on your computer, but on remote computers called servers. When you want to use the file, your computer simply connects to the server through the Internet. This means you can access the same files using any computer.

Timeline of the Computer

1939

Alan Turing's bombe computer is used to crack German codes during World War II.

1977

The Apple II computer is released.

At Your Fingertips

The introduction of touch screen technology has made it easier to operate a computer. All users need to do is tap and drag their fingers on a screen. One of the first touch screen smartphones, IBM's Simon, was released in 1994. However, the device wasn't popular. It wasn't until the 2007 launch of Apple's iPhone that these handy devices caught on with the general public.

2010
The first Apple iPad hits stores.

21st Century
Developers continue to improve computers, investigating artificial intelligence.

1985
Microsoft releases the first version of its Windows operating system.

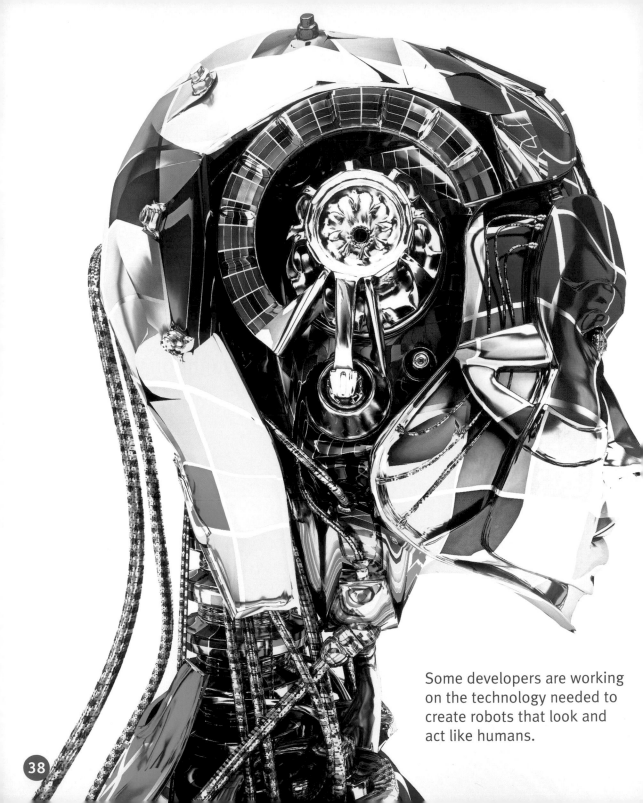

Some developers are working on the technology needed to create robots that look and act like humans.

The Future of Computing

As common as computers already are, they are likely to play an even larger role in our lives in the future. Many home appliances and electronic devices, from refrigerators to lighting systems, can already be connected to the Internet and controlled using a phone or tablet. Soon, a computer might control almost every object in your home.

Computers may one day be controlled by eye or body movement.

Behind the Wheel

Even your car might be computer controlled in the future. Many of today's cars already rely on computer systems for many features. These systems control the temperature inside the car, turn on our headlights, and even give us directions. But what if a computer was completely in control of steering and navigating your car? Self-driving cars that can anticipate and react to traffic conditions are already being tested. Such technology may reduce the number of traffic accidents due to distracted drivers or other causes.

Self-driving cars created by Google use cameras, computers, and satellites to navigate without human drivers.

Thinking for Themselves

The future of computers may lie in artificial intelligence (AI). Scientists believe they can duplicate human intelligence and create computers that can think for themselves. As far back as 1950, researchers at Dartmouth College demonstrated software that could beat humans at games of chess.

Two robots compete in a game of chess in 2014.

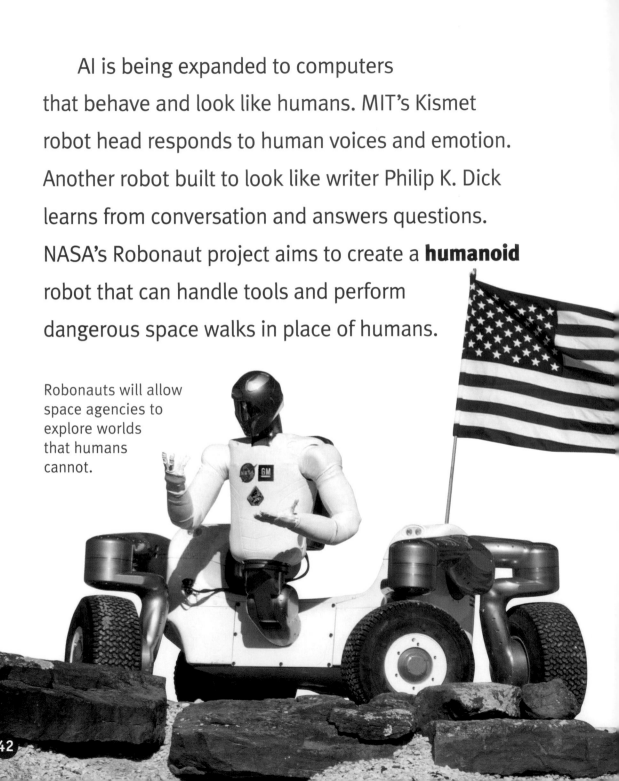

AI is being expanded to computers that behave and look like humans. MIT's Kismet robot head responds to human voices and emotion. Another robot built to look like writer Philip K. Dick learns from conversation and answers questions. NASA's Robonaut project aims to create a **humanoid** robot that can handle tools and perform dangerous space walks in place of humans.

Robonauts will allow space agencies to explore worlds that humans cannot.

Robots are often made to look or act like living creatures such as this drone insect.

What's Next?

Some scientists and philosophers worry about the role computers play in our lives. They think computers may soon substitute for developing our own intelligence. The machines would simply do everything for us. Would this be more helpful to humanity or more harmful? Could computers replace humans completely? Will they eventually look, speak, and even think and act like us? If you were in charge, how far would you go? ★

True Statistics

Number of pieces used to build the first computer: 25,000

Number of cables used to build ENIAC: 6,200

Number of worldwide Internet users in 2015: 3 billion

Number of personal computers in use in 2015: 15 billion

Number of personal computers in the United States today: 311 million

Number of personal computers in China today: 195 million

Smallest computer: The University of Michigan's Micro Mote

Did you find the truth?

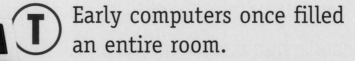 Microsoft invented the first personal computers.

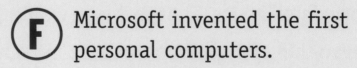 Early computers once filled an entire room.

Resources

Books

Mara, Wil. *Software Development: Science, Technology, Engineering*. New York: Children's Press, 2016.

Ventura, Marne. *The 12 Biggest Breakthroughs in Computer Technology*. North Mankato, MN: 12-Story Library, 2015.

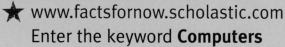

Visit this Scholastic Web site for more information on computers:
★ www.factsfornow.scholastic.com
Enter the keyword **Computers**

Important Words

humanoid (HYOO-muh-noyd) something that has the shape and appearance of a human

input (IN-put) to feed information into a computer

integrated circuits (IN-tuh-gray-tid SUR-kits) pieces of plastic that have electrical circuits printed on them in the form of small metal strips

network (NET-wurk) a group of connected computers or other communications equipment

operating system (AH-pur-ay-ting SIS-tuhm) software in a computer that supports all the programs that run on it

programming language (PROH-gram-ing LANG-wij) a language used to create instructions for a computer

rotors (ROH-turz) parts of a machine that turn or rotate

semiconductor (sem-ee-kuhn-DUK-tuhr) a substance that doesn't conduct electricity well at low temperatures but whose conductivity improves at higher temperatures

software (SAWFT-wair) computer programs that control the workings of the equipment, or hardware, and direct it to do specific tasks

supercomputers (SOO-pur-kuhm-pyoo-turz) large and extremely powerful computers used mainly for scientific tasks

trigonometry (trig-uh-NAH-muh-tree) a branch of math that focuses on the angles of triangles